The Delicate Falling of a God

ROSHAN DOUG

UCE Press

The Delicate Falling of a God

Roshan Doug is a Visiting Professor in Poetry at the University of Central England. He is also the Resident Poet at the Repertory Theatre, Birmingham.

First published in 2003
by
UCE Press
University of Central England
Perry Barr, Birmingham B42 2SU
United Kingdom
Distributed by Marketing Unit

Typeset by L. Simmonds

Printed by The Bath Press
Lower Bristol Road, Bath BA2 3BL
United Kingdom

A CIP record for this book is available from the
British Library

ISBN 0-90435457-1

Acknowledgements

I would like to thank the BBC for commissioning and broadcasting poems which appear in this collection, and newspapers including, *The Independent*, *The Times*, *The Times Educational Supplement* and *The Sunday Times of India*. 'Time Passed Like Fever' was commissioned by the Birmingham Repertory Theatre; 'This is Where Your Guru Stood' was broadcast as part of a programme on India, *A Land of Ghosts, Dreams and Goblins* broadcast on BBC Radio 4; 'When the War Broke Out' was first broadcast on *Something Understood* and, 'A Vertical Construct' was commissioned by the University of Central England on the first anniversary of the events of 11th September.

I would also like to thank the following for their boundless encouragement in the production of this collection: Laura Parfitt at Unique Broadcasting Company and Jonathan Church, Artistic Director at the Birmingham Repertory Theatre, Professor Philip Walkling, Pro-Vice Chancellor at the University of Central England, for his support and sponsorship; the Indian High Commissioner, Ronen Sen, for recognising the importance of poetry to promote cultural understanding, and Samina Liaquat and my son, Suneil, for listening to my perpetual and, sometimes, rather deranged thoughts on life and philosophy.

Finally, I would like to thank Lynne Simmonds, my colleague, friend and confidante for guiding and helping me to put this collection together.

For Anjana and Vinesh

CONTENTS

The Delicate Falling of a God

The unmentionable odour of death
Offends the September night.

W.H. Auden
(September 1 1939) from Another Time, 1940

I

I was driving home that day from Gloucestershire – had just hit the M5 at Bristol trying to keep an eye on the road ahead, the traffic, and wiping away raindrops in a clear blue sky which were falling upon the cacophony of twenty-first century Christendom. I had been recording something or other at the BBC on Whiteladies Road near Black Boy Hill, had had lunch near the suspension bridge overlooking the mammoth ridge etched above a gateway to the underworld or not, of history, poetry and the BBC.

And as I made my way onto the motorway, it seems incredible to me now that I was inert and oblivious to all that was about to unfold around me, preoccupied by my own performance at the studio, as if I were the centre of the universe, that the stars stood for me like spotlights and that I could control them at will, by acting, by moving on a stage as if my chance and its coming round is my choice, determined by me and me alone.

And in that self-satisfied state, hedonistic turmoil, I flittered from one thought to another, rather like an undefined consciousness, a trail that was leading to nowhere but to myself.

Abruptly the news flash on the radio, tangled words about New York, a plane and the World Trade Centre. Suddenly the clouds gathered around me like an omen of some kind, a prowling beast moving towards me. And then within a distance of no more than ten miles, there's repetition, another plane, and *terrorism* breaks out, a word more deadly than ever before as if touching my world for the first time and Islamic fundamentalists standing in a surreal panoramic vision.

All of a sudden it wasn't the Middle East then, but New York as if, for the first time, our realities were really colliding.

They say that sometimes you can glimpse or feel a future you didn't plan or see. At that moment, I saw something unholy, as if history had come and gone and had left no distinguishing mark or impression on our perception of reason or logic. It was all dry and useless, unperturbed like soot that had built up over hundreds of years.

And I remember looking up and sensing the sky standing motionless, the world not breathing, as if hearing the next stage in the movement of the universe. And I had this inexplicable urge to speak on the mobile phone, to listen for comfort. All I wanted was to hear your voice, a simple utterance of familiarity because for years we had lived without living, merely existing as extras waiting at the wings of a grand stage. In your voice I knew I'd be able to feel a sense of now, self and place. But nothing came.

In seconds, like the turning of a leaf, I watched the looming battle of the gods and ideologies, and the world dividing. The arena set for a grand finale.

II

A vertical construct
is a skyscraper,
each block a frame
of our lives,
our security.
And when it crumbles
through a belief –
or half-belief –
I see Man
as a dream,
quiet and frail,
like the delicate falling
of a god.

III

For all that we do, we pray -

Pray
this plane that takes us to the sky
will bring us back home
safe and sound
gently to the ground.

Pray
that as Time leads us on
we live our lives growing old
side by side
like a carousel ride.

though nothing comes of it.

IV

Our school bell was a tiny sound, which I recall, faint and sickly like the reaching out of dreams that New York embodied for me at the age of fifteen when desperately I wanted to act on Broadway.

I sat there week after week in my geography class focusing on *The Political Map of the World* above the chalk-drenched board lettered with boredom. But Mr. James would occasionally allow me to drift into another world in the haze of the chalk dust that filtered in the sun-stream, as if I was a lost soul in a trance out of touch with my class unaware of proper speech or the sad hypnotic ringing of the bell – calling for me like history, that haunts your consciousness or like a dark unforeseeable tragedy that was yet to invade our language.

V

Oh, Time
upon whose hands
we dream of heaven –
this way and that,
from this star to this,
in a millionth of a second,
searching for the One –
guide us out of this hole,
this dank so dark,
this death so deep,
and show us
how it feels
to be a human form,
that contented
fallen thing,
once again –
washed with the tide
flowing with the waves –
those watery strands
that govern our life,
our being
and all our innocence.

VI

When I look into the autumn clouds
I sometimes see *forgiveness*

spreading out against the dusky sky
and *sorry* appearing like a rainbow.

It was like that time
you had an abortion

in that private
clinic, so late –

Something good will come of this,
you said. Perhaps you're right,

something good will come of this
one day, some day, one fine day.

7

VII

Just think
all this

one day
all this

fading
into thin air

not a stone
or a brick

in sight
not a tear

nor a word
just think

all this
all of it

ascending
with the rising dust

only your look
our children

and these words
remaining

forever

like evidence

of a dying
world

that's crumbling
like a relic

of a by-gone age
or language

(Latin or Sanskrit)
that ceases to be,

or gets distorted
by history

id est the way
Himmler

(with the aid
of Ernst Schäfer)

linked lingual
patterns

for his own
grand purpose –

that theory,
the survival of

the fittest gone

mad.

For *ayran*
read *arya*.

Yes, we're
talking

about extinction,
dear.

Let me say it again
x-tink-shun.

VIII

Wa maa huwa bi-qawli saa-'ir: qaliilam-maa tu'- min-uun!
'It is not poet's speech – little is it that ye believe!'
The Koran, LXIX, *The Reality*

In the beginning was a plane
and the plane was heading towards a god.

In that god was a word
and the word was *love* but no one knew it

and the word was blown to bits
just like our god and all his poets

right down to ashes or a funeral pyre
ignited by a Colt.45 automatic,

pure fictionality, absolutely,
pure as it is or was, or can be –

like an empty bin liner
bouncing in the wind,

the offending of your god –
that flicker to death,

that sin forming and renewing –
in the deafness of the breeze.

IX

If your book is full of words
give me a word

to soothe away
all my hopes

of yesterdays.
Give me a word

that explains
what I see

what this means,
where God is

if God *is* at all,
blessing this

this mass of chaos
unfolding.

Give me a word
to help me see

beyond all this,
beyond this world

flickering in time
like a funeral pyre

and everything,

all our follies,

swarming around
like cells

in the vessels
of the universe,

the dark frozen
depths

of our blighted
souls

which some say
speak to us

in the obscure
deadness of the night,

that *midnight
moment's forest*

when language
penetrates

all our awakenings
Gas, Gas, Quick boys!

from the classroom
to the field;

from the obscurity

of science

to the long power
of poetry.

X

Who said, *do not go gentle into the good night*?
That's just poetry.

All around it's rage I see
rage, rage, rage.

But thoughts of you gentles me
just a little

when the rain falls and sun shines
like memories of all we are

a Sunni Muslim, a crazed Shiite
or an emerging shibboleth.

And though *the light has gone
out of our lives*

and darkness is everywhere
I will use

the only arms of defence:
silence, exile and cunning

like a torch in a forest
full of death and mosquitoes.

And the faint echo of your breathing
touches me

like joss-stick scent

in a dark *puja* room,

full of secret hopes
in a dying world.

XI

I'll weigh these words
in the palm of my hand

to see what they are
and how this fits in

with everything I know
of education.

Guide me out of this,
you stars

because my god
is falling from the sky

landing between *jihad*
and the *crusades*

where philosophy
doesn't exist

and human beings
paint themselves like you

delving deep
a million miles in space

where no-one speaks
and an echo

drifts, like a surreal

dream –

a backdrop (the outline)
in a film or a play,

a stinking stench
of deadness, decay or fish.

XII

'Wa 'innahuu Iaqaasamul – law ta '-lamuuna 'aziim,'
'Nay, I swear by the places of the stars,'
The Koran, LVI, The Event

It's nothing personal
these bombs

just an exercise
in surrealism;

the placing of a butterfly
next to a katipo.

Bombs and food
for you and your god

for you and me
and this our tiny world

shining out from the dark
which you call *home*,

like conscience
overwrought, clearly.

And all your words and books
illuminating

like reality
in a different world

redefined in a poem,
to rebuild.

So what will there be
when you have gone?

Just the rubble, the dust
and smoke

your god, my god
and all our lives

drifting passed
the boundaries of eternity –

an instant that we are
and here where we live –

taking rubble to rubble,
dust to dust

and with them
all our ashes.

XIII

This hand which you clutch
takes me to the walls of Palestine and Kashmir
and reminds me
that death is
a permanent part of our consciousness –

no matter what we believe
or strive to be.

And each tightening of a grip
takes us close (*even* closer)
to what is to come
and bellows to distance theocracy,
our world and everything in it,
including you and our cold infelicity.

XIV

I never thought we'd go like this
our world tested

and all that we stand for
plunging into concrete –

with only the belief
that love is eternity

and that perhaps,
just perhaps,

our philosophy
and our concept of high

divinity may or
may not be what it seems

despite what Reverend Burnell
said in R.E., that word

missionary, purifying
the pages of my text book,

the cold touchstone
of our hemisphere,

the ice blueprints
of our dreams, or politics.

XV

'...two opposing cultures are pushed like plates of the Earth's crust.'
Brenda Maddox, The Guardian, 28th September 2001

Call me not your books,
not a sentence

or a word.
Speak not the language,

not the tongue
of an ancient world

where gods excelled
and wars were waged

upon nations
and empires that ruled

the universe.
Don't call me a Muslim,

a Christian or a Jew.
Call me by my name

quietly, Uncle Tom.
Let me see myself

and remind me again
of who I am

soundlessly away from

this conflict,

where there's opening of the earth
and the world gapes,

like a foreign entity
widening out

forever into blackness,
a hole

going on, going deep
and never quite ending.

XVI

For Anjana

Quietly we play building this tower
to the sky.

Your face, a picture of careful
concentration.

You place your blocks gently,
softly like innocence

on wafer-thin ground
whilst clutching my hand for guidance.

Your contorted smile,
your deftly silence.

And then at last, you rise
like a whispered prayer,

tiptoeing across the floor –
hoping the tower won't fall.

XVII

At the dentist I flick through last year's magazines
and read the horoscope to take my mind off the
    drilling
and filling that are coming.

Patients sit there patiently doing the same.

An old woman walks in smiling
and starts talking to another woman seated next to me.
They talk jovially as if they haven't heard the news,

as if New York last night was a cinematic
    reproduction,
a fictional aspect of our reality,
in the dark depths of space

where no-one dies and no-one worries a bit.

XVIII

We sit ominously
soft and aimless

for the ticket machine
to get to seventy-seven

when my father's turn
will come up

like an awakening
in the dark,

and a needle will puncture
a cold extraction

of red, the linkage
of life and lineage.

And in that moment
that body will snap

a sample from
two thirds of water

to be placed like a drug
under the microscopic eye

of medicine or language
that records our life

slow as a timepiece

in the A & E.

And then a heartbeat,
a movement

a reminder of our cold
existence,

our hopes, our thoughts
and all we are

thumping down
like a sentence decreed

by an English judge
in an English court

where fate loiters
in the corridors of uncertainty.

XIX

'The courage of life is often a less dramatic spectacle than the courage of a final moment; but is no less a magnificent mixture of triumph and tragedy.'
John F. Kennedy, Profiles In Courage, 1957

Time passed like fever whilst you stood at the wings,
that night,

your face was a radiant of death or illness.
You listened

minutely for your cue, unmarked, unscripted
which

you'd learnt like the signs of the zodiac and had
    repeated
obsessively

for the previous seven weeks when you were bathing
in poetry.

How many years did you wait for that moment
that stood

before you then? It was quiet and still, words across
    time.
Abruptly it came

like a call, brief and invisible, beckoning you to life,
the half-life

and the living – the fame, the glitter, the immeasurable
applause.

XX

'There is a land of the living and a land of the dead, and the bridge is love.'
Tony Blair quoting Thorton Wilder on 20th September 2001 at the memorial service in New York

Do you remember when we first kissed
or that time when I told you

I love you?
That moment so rare, so light

you thought I'd forgotten it,
didn't you?

A couple of years before
we'd sat at the Crown and Angel

at the corner of St. Martin's Lane
and New Row

(near Covent Garden)
in a state of giddy-stupor

and then wandered around
in the National Gallery.

You laughed uncontrollably
at 'The Execution of Lady Jane Grey'

when I had said,
'It's forever in my mind.'

You were loud like a school girl

30

on an outing.

'Forever?' you repeated
 in your Lancashire drawl,

'What do you mean, *forever*?'
and giggled teasingly –

your rosy cheeks, your freckles
and red hair.

I'm at that point now on the edge
of that word *forever* and I'm about

to see the fabrics of this world
and this thing we call *finality,*

like the taking of the seed of life,
our choice. My heart has grown,

like the spirit of Lady Jane Grey.
And as I fall, all around

I see the fading away of light,
the lifting of a *burka* –

the clarity of an illusion –
where water glides

like a paper plane carrying
our hopes, a sense

of *otherness*. And in that airiness,

that lightness of blue,

is a bold link, call it *love,*
that bridge we've built,

between the living and the dead
like that painting hanging

violently in the Gallery
conveying a romanticized

vision of *Englishness* –
not abstract but divine actuality.

XXI

It's the absurdity of life,
this belief (yes *belief*),
that some gods really care

when all around
it's true
they don't.

Take my son with asthma –
undefined by mercy.

And look at this,
this plane heading towards Babylon –
a fireball of a philosophy
or what you call, belief –
*dis*belief.

My son with eczema –
unperturbed, unaccustomed to curse.

So what kind of gods are *these*
and who are we
to believe they *care?*

No one does.
Except the turnsoles you've planted
in the backyard, leaning,

inexplicably, towards the sun –
not explained by reason or learning –
giving hope to a lie

or to the essence of a truth

like pure magic.

XXII

At the bus stop a peroxide girl squints in the fading
    sun.
A portly old man inhales the filter-close cigarette –
the last breath of life.

Over the road a prayer class has just finished.

Shalwar-kameezed children stream out of the building,
clutching their copies of *The Koran* or not.
They're loud and voluble – over taken with relief.

And only a single girl, quietly abashed,
smiles at the descending dusk – like a thought in the
    making
or cajoling to find itself.

XXIII

'The cradle rocks above an abyss...'
Vladmir Nabokov, Speak, Memory, 1951

Everyday I felt I was falling into the abyss
of neurosis not knowing how or why
I came to be who I was.

And then I saw you and we talked
the night before I heard the news on the radio
that the world was crumbling to bits.

And I described you as a huddling old hag,
your face falling apart loosening like a rubbery
thing. You cried, I remember.

And then we lay silent for much of the night.
Even dawn appeared like *a brief crack of light*
between two eternities of darkness.

It's the taking away of you from me
from life and history, like perfection
as if the light had revealed all.

And not all my apologies could save you
from the graveyard of our relationship
where truth should never be acknowledged.

XXIV

I heard an old story about reincarnation
about a man who came back as a tree.

He (or *it*) is still there in a remote part of Canada,
(according to my mother's pundit)

trapped between the life in this world
and the memories of its former atrocities.

It wails late at night, he said, *as if seeking
a call from a divine being.*

I thought of this that night when the storm
blew down our oak tree back in '87.

It came crashing down on the shed you had
bought on a visit to the country.

And it lay there for weeks
before we did something about it.

Do you remember it?
Perhaps that was some kind of a god

releasing the life of that tree,
and *forgiveness* which we couldn't allow

was brought inexplicably through the storm.
But if the gods were happy

(and there was nothing to suppose

they weren't) then who were we,

the size of an ocean drop,
stuck in a plan, to complain they don't care?

XXV

You could have created something
deeper than what you did

but you didn't;
you medalled yourself a hero.

You could have taken
a buttermilk sandwich

and washed it down with honey
and then sighed with relief

to say we've done it,
we've conquered it all.

Instead we're swarmed
in the desolate air,

that deep drowning
deadness

where the sun shines
like a god, or demigod

and occasional crumbs
fall from the sky,

like the kaokaoing
of the gulls.

So nothing much to see now

but oil, bombs and lust;

nothing worth dying for
but oil, sand and dust.

XXVI

'...you have to believe God has a plan.'
Mayor of New York, **Rudolph Giulian**

Occasionally in our lives, once in while, we come
across a whirlwind from our cold frailties that speaks
and shocks and reminds us of who we really are – not
the kangaroo-court we're in.

So smear your face and nose,
butter your finger nail,
bless your friend and foe,
this world it has to fail.

And then it vanishes into thin air like confetti on Flag
Day – the stuff of kind democracy, a glossy gathering,
a stream of pageantry, lords and ladies, kings and
queens, gods and all. But it's an illusion unobtainable
like timelessness and infinity.

So shape it as it's falling,
point an iron rod,
hear your conscience calling,
and never speak of God.

XXVII

'Home'? What is that word 'Home'?
Richard Bach, 1977

This is where your guru stood
your inspiration,
at the end of this cobblestone alley –
when he gave you a glimpse
of your future world, my world.

You were only six or seven
that night when you saw Him –
a beam of light had lit his head
whilst you played hide and seek
or its equivalent in a Punjabi universe.

And this, my prayer is just a prayer
not unique or personified *dis*belief,
not the finding of a god or my home,
in this your alleyway.

I've merely come to pay my respects,
to you and your guru, to your village,
to your array of stories
which I believe or half believe –

not knowing how or why
we've never quite fitted in,
not in the idolised past you've built
or Britain in your dying world.

XXVIII

There are words I wish I'd said
words from another world

when I left that morning.
But nothing came to me.

Just a grunt, the mumbling
of a familiar phrase

that had lost its potency.
The details of our world

stuck throughout that day –
your mundane routine,

my lifeless actions
and our constant inactions –

and stood emphatically
like a herd of white elephants

in which the clarity of a vision
of the inner-self is all.

It's that point of parting
when the epiphany –

what you call 'the truth'–
is the answer to all our being

my dry wanderings,

my untested philosophies

of my way and life
that lead climactically to you.

XXIX

'A photograph...is a trace, something directly stencilled off the real, like a footprint or a death mask.'
Susan Sontag, New York Review of Books, 23rd June 1977

Nothing stays the same
not as it is
not as it was

as if our disasters
are reminders
of our vulnerability

when they touch
our perceptions
of ourselves –

like photographs –
that stick
in the memory bank

and tug at the cold frailty
of our lives
as if the universe

will engulf us,
swallow us up
in its timeless bang

the distant hollowness
of space –
traced off or erased

like indecipherable reality,

a cheap animation
something close to foreign

like a footprint of life
quietly subdued
serene as an old man

draped in a *doti*
in the early Indian morn.
And all standing still.

XXX

'...the sunset would deepen through cinnamon to aubergine,'
Paul Muldoon, Gathering Mushrooms, 1983

'The world is an oyster,' they say,
though to be honest,
it's more like turmeric *keema*
cooked on a clay oven in the midday heat,
where the sizzling *ghee*, garlic-onions and green
   chillies,
echo nothing but Mogul history.

Remember that night we got caught in the monsoon?
You slept motionless
as if you weren't breathing
as if your conscience was clear
like a *moolie*
or the water from the tube-wells in the fields
of rice, pure white,
in the village of Adampur.

Your touch stretched high into the ceiling
and your breath, the spirit of an ancient princess,
was warm and historic,
the taste of *kedgeree*.

All night I remember I listened to your silence;
our distant promises.
And the sound of the rain on a hot tin roof.

XXXI

We don't even own the breath
we take

or comprehend the mechanism
that embraces it.

So now, just think, my love,
how can we hope to understand

the grand scheme of things
when we're too busy

creating gods, one by one
as demons of our daily lives

misunderstood by many
like compound words and apostrophes?

Or how aesthetics and art
can align themselves with atrocities

like Mata Hari's dance
watched by the Nazi generals,

or how Nietzsche's philosophising
inspires Hitler and his doings.

XXXII

'In what language do you think?'
Question in a Swiss Census form

Let's just say this
this for the last time
the last time
this word you loved
let's just say this
this again and this
for a thousand wishes
let's just say this
just this
for the very last time
and nothing else
as if there's
nothing else at all
let's just say this
this word
you've taken to bed
that arouses you
aligns you with
citizenship
or nationality
(whichever means most
on a passport)
let's just say
this word *English*
whatever you perceive
it to be
as if it will hand you
a set of values
which you can embrace

or reject
and your conscience
will be clear
as a crystal ball –
lingual sovereignty
and choice
nothing wrong
with choices, my dear,
it's all part of the trick
pick a card
any card …
and here we are
back at this word
which means so much
and so much that means
sod all.

XXXIII

Not me, sir, not me. It wasn't me at all.
Not when I knew what I was doing,
what I was taking on, what I was becoming.
I only went with them half-heartedly
lead somewhat cautiously, quietly.

Yes, I went following them blindly
because they promised me so much
they promised too much –
martyrdom and eternity not death
not at that point, not then.

Judge or no judge, care or fictionality –
facts clouded with prejudice.
It's death penalty.

Lambs to the slaughter, lambs to the slaughter
we are as time moves on eternally
and only then the desperate bleating of our cries –

the buildings of Dresden and Belsen,
the remnants of our cold history.

XXXIV

When the war broke out...

The quiet buzz of the radio
woke me last night –
the intermittent sounds of news, words
and music
bombarding my subconscious mind.

It's the underworld neither here nor there,
just being,
trying to make sense
of this surface reality.

Language came flooding from a midnight sky –
'the imminent' had arrived,
'the inevitable' –
sound bites and political gloss
paving the way now
for fictionality.

'Pictures are coming in',
'the offensive has begun',
'Baghdad woke up to air-raid sirens',
'diplomacy had given way to action'.

Indeed.

And this narrative is intercepted
with a climax,
this 'final scene'
juxtaposed with an array of voices,

reminding us of what has been.

Here's our correspondent in Washington/Kuwait',
'analysis',
'John or Sally with our troops'
and 'Finally...'

Images came to my mind of chess pieces and cricket,
of time moving on,
and still we're static,
despite the arts, the guiding scholars
and thousands of poets.

In my head, George Bush (addressing his nation)
and Saddam Hussein (addressing his nation)
stood defiantly
like characters in the grand scheme
of a play.

Amidst all this, the notes of *The Moonlight Sonata*
filtered through
touching our hope for humanity.

But oh, Time, cover me and all mankind
for the faint tolling of the bell reminds me,
it's tolling for me.

XXXV

'...art shows us something about where we are, what we share, what divides us, the cruelties we commit...'
Adrian Searle, The Guardian

You can lead a horse to water
but you can't
for the life of the world
understand the strange complexities
that govern the human mind
like how it is
that this or that came into being
or what this means
if it has a meaning at all
('cause everything has a meaning).
So what now,
that we have blown life to smithereens?
Only the buzzing of the news on CNN
portrays our truths;
only the fluttering of folly and remorse
flicker in the midday heat
where the youths stand purposefully
their hearts ticking
like a song or an imminent bomb
whichever comes first (or last?)
to entice their growing conscience
(or conscious*ness*)
in history, life and politics
in spite of, or as a result of,
'the cruelties we commit'
hidden away by politics –
our crimes safe in our beards.

XXXVI

The rattle of your bangles
and your gold jewellery on the windowsill
woke me that night.

I looked out.
The window ajar in the breeze.

In the darkness the rain fell
drumming incessantly
like the faint calling of a god.

Such was the night.

I could have heard a million voices
clashing with a million gods
defining *clarity* and all that we call *is*.

But I didn't.
I only felt your breathing.

You lay fast asleep like a child
oblivious to the beckoning
of that dying world
crumbling down with the rain.

And I huddled up beside you
as if your touch,
or the contours of your hips,
could cleanse humanity of its sins.

XXXVII

I've decided that I'm going to exchange
my identity for the one defined

by my credit card company –
financial institutions

always know better than us
as to who we are, what we'll earn

and what we can afford.
But keeping up with my new adopted role

is a bit of a strain.
Even my signature is becoming lopsided

falling down from the line
and difficult to keep upright

as if my hands
have become independent of my will.

My choice is not *my* choice.
It's my fate designed by the omnipotent gods

with slick-coloured ties, seated in plush carpeted
    rooms
behind windows with blinds

where money falls from the sky
like confetti on an Indian wedding night.

XXXVIII

The spider was crawling gently
towards the web

after sensing the fluttering fly
caught in the centre

desperate to escape its
inevitable end

that was clearly
drawing in.

I watched with an infant
fascination

how it was going
to be eaten up

and wondered if
perhaps,

before he ate the fly,
there'd be

a split second pause
granted by the spider,

a kind of a divine instinct
inherent in nature

which would provide

a chance for the minute-ist form

to redeem itself –
from life and all its sins.

XXXIX

We were on a late night train
from Calais to Paris.

You were finishing the half eaten
ham sandwich

we had bought from Waterloo
when out of the blue,

in mid-joke, you paused
as if someone had stepped

over your grave, and your bones
were grinding to dust.

They say that sometimes
we sense a future we didn't plan

arbitrary to all that we call
reason and logic

lying strategically
between life and half-light

like a full moon when
clarity and magic are all,

a sight you can sense,
a brightness,

even in that lull

that cold solitude of the night.

You never did finish that joke
or the ham sandwich

and I remember your eyes
had dropped as if something

deep, whole and abstract
had died inside you.

And amidst the drone
of the engine

and the sadness of your eyes,
we stared out of the window

at the lonely darkness –
reaching to hope

or a promise
in the unmentionable stars –

and a benign universe,
forever changing.

XL

The dog with three legs
limped slowly

with his blind owner
tugging at his lead.

It was Sunday again
as I watched

them returning
from the local church

at the back of our house
(visible over the fence).

That evening I thought of them
sitting there

praying thanks for all
that a god had given them

and I wondered who
was blessed with whom

giving divine gratitude
a meaning of its own

by living a destiny
uniquely and alone,

in a universe that excludes

justice, sense and sensibility.

XLI

England

Wet wintry weather blows like a breeze
in this cruel, acid autumn –
untouched by words or foreign explantations.

But I know that flowers rise, bloom and die;
winter falls and spring returns
and youth is an instant away.

Iraq

And there are boys I know, sunk,
who sit by the road
with the sun beating down on them.

And their bloodshot eyes are the world
of yours and mine
and they dream the colours of our currency.

XLII

I sat on the toilet for the seventh time, pondering;
what would we have said

knowing we'd never see each other again?
There are words unsaid –

I regret –
and words I should never have said

that fell from my lips like a bad omen
quietly like the dripping of blood

whilst Allah and my god stood talking.

XLIII

On the execution of a Buddhist monk, Yodchat Suapoo, convicted of
mugging, rape and murder

When you watch me die
and the judge has made no call,
and the clock ticks to twelve,
just make sure my young blood
doesn't spill on the floor;
a thousand bullets will zip by
but don't let it fall;
let it drip on a pillow
or the cushion of your breast
but not on wood,
not on the rubble or the sand
that lies on the floor;
don't let it splatter underneath the feet that now
support a cat, a dog, a rat
but my hot blood has no value no more;
let not those drunkards tread on me
with their vomit and mindless worth;
hold out your palm
and interlock every drip and drop that falls;
I'm the son of an celestial name;
I'm the glint of morning dew;
I'm the colours of the rainbow;
call out Neptune and the tidal waves;
his laughing at me (I know);
pray to that star that shines
that it may lift me to its side
or let it gush my soul to the earth born stream
to melt my form to wind;
hold me if you please,

decompose me if you must
but don't let my blood fall on the floor;
hide me in a temple, lock me in a cave;
take a snap while I breathe
of Thailand and its breeze;
call out the lava to rise;
let the mountains hear your sighs;
let the churches crumble to the ground,
drift in an everlasting
dust of airs and blasts and doom;
I'm eternally damned to death
and my soul now swoons.
But don't let my blood spill on the floor.

XLIV

'No, I read no Poetry now; it might soften me.'
Field Marshal Paul von Hindenberg

If I believe that you're real,
all this, that this is love,
if I believe that you're mine
and life is a gentle dove...

The house was silent for quite sometime as we watched those feats of engineering crumbling down. The shock and horror of the sight froze us like icicles on a washing line in January. We looked on, numb with disbelief, not knowing the causes of how and why, what philosophy was, where it had been and how we all fitted in.

And still there was no sound.

Images came and went, searing the retina deep in the confines of our world as pictures played and replayed, sometimes in silence, sometimes with commentary and occasionally in slow motion as if a frame of the reel might reveal something about the workings of that illusion, an exploration underneath our surface reality, the dissecting of a metrical rhythm, the central point of a heartbeat.

My mother went into the *puja* room filled with joss-stick smoke to do the evening *arti* and spent a lot longer than before, as if the quality of a prayer is dependent on its length and can flutter itself into the hands of a god. She placed a sunflower and a rose I

had given her for her birthday – her wish – next to
Hanuman and Krishna, a gift from this world, placing
all that she knew, all that she was (and we were), into
the wings of fate. She continued for days after that, an
earnest ritual she exercised like second nature, all
mechanised and perfected, assisted by a range of
flowers and sweets. But I knew it wasn't for us, her
family, but for humanity this time, the world and all
its sins.

Slowly we felt a movement, a tremor, a kind of
awakening from sobriety, as if we'd been comatosed
for centuries. Daylight came through. Outside the
autumn sun fell and rose as it had for countless years.
Nothing changed. And then, within a week,
something spoke, nudging us into action, to alertness.
Our education and logic subsiding from view. And
cold anger emerged.
- *Wanted dead or alive, let's smoke them out...*
Fictionality interjected with reality both in words and
in deeds. It was a sense of calling that's both urgent
and dramatic. And an animal instinct getting the
better of us, the sound and fury. On our screens we
saw leaders standing tall, side by side, united against
some common enemies, death and vanity. And the
workings of an ego. We looked on, instinctively but
clearly mute, listening to speech after speech,
defending a call to arms – a bugle call, clashing
against the faint tolling of the bell.
- *To do nothing is the irresponsible thing.*
To do something, anything was paramount. Let words
speak, and all our thoughts mould into a ball of fire,
for *Readiness was all.*

And we were, all ready. For now it was all revenge, conscience and action colliding like real entities. Ancient gods came out and battled on sovereign ground and celestial bodies moved, rose and died simultaneously, some wide, some narrow, and others not quite forming. And all our crimes in our beards stood like a full moon, all clear, all clarity. And I imagined that they were somewhere in that outer space, just being, as if their presence was all, and all was everything.

- *Action, Hamlet, Action!*

And I remember one night when my mother sat in the *puja* room, slumped like a sack. She was meditating or had fallen asleep. In the dark she stood out, like a vessel, a body without a spirit or a soul, a keel yearning to find its way back to the universe, the cycle of life and our beginning. And the tear on her cheek, static and motionless, was the size of the world. Next to her the sunflower and the sickly rose lay – wilting in a hope filled room, all promises, all wishes – as if they too had failed like us and my mother's tear that had died in mid-stream.

- *Hari Rama, hari Krishna, hari Krishna, hari, hari...*

On the screen voices converged as if our life and history depended on it, as if we'd gone back in time and the past, that abstract thought from school, was a physical entity, all relevant. From an aerial view, the end was nigh, a mere moment away, and death was a flicker of reality.

Only your words echoed through, my comfort, like a distant call, a desolate song:

...If I believe in your words
and Time crossing the sea,
why is it that I also believe
that Hope will never find me?

7